HOW TO PROVIDE GREAT CUSTOMER SERVICE

Master the Art of Customer Care

Ray Goodwin

CONTENTS

LIABILITY DISCLAIMER

The information contained within this book is intended for informational purposes only and should not be construed as legal or professional advice. The authors and publishers of this book are not responsible for any losses or damages that may arise from the use of the information contained within.

The reader assumes full responsibility for any decisions made based on the information in this book. The authors and publishers do not endorse any particular method, service or product mentioned in this book and are not responsible for any consequences resulting from their use.

The reader should exercise caution and discretion when making life changing decisions, and should be aware of the risks and potential consequences of their actions. This book is not a substitute for professional or legal advice and should not be relied upon as such.

By reading and using the information in this book, the reader acknowledges and agrees to hold harmless the authors, publishers, and any other parties involved in the creation or distribution of this book from any and all liability, claims, damages, or losses that may arise from their use of the information contained herein.

CHAPTER 1: INTRODUCTION TO CUSTOMER SERVICE

Welcome to "How to Provide Great Customer Service" – the definitive guide to creating happy customers and building a thriving business. In today's world, where competition is fierce and consumer expectations are higher than ever before, it's essential to have strong customer service skills that can help set you apart from the crowd.

As an author with over 25 years of experience in online sales, I've learned first-hand that providing great customer service is crucial for success in any industry. Whether you own a small business or work for a large corporation, your ability to make customers feel valued and appreciated can make all the difference.

In this book, we'll explore practical and actionable strategies that will help you build strong relationships with your customers. From understanding their needs and preferences to addressing complaints and resolving conflicts, we'll cover everything you need to know about delivering top-notch service that keeps your customers coming back.

But great customer service isn't just good for business – it's also good for you! By providing excellent customer service, you'll not only improve your bottom line but also enhance your personal satisfaction as well.

So if you're ready to take your customer service skills to the next level, join me on this journey towards excellence!

In today's highly competitive business landscape, customer service can make or break a business. Providing exceptional customer service has become the key to retaining loyal customers and generating strong referrals for any business.

The Importance of Customer Service to Businesses

Customer service has been the backbone of successful businesses for many years. In today's world, however, it has become even more important. Customers have a broad range of options to choose from, from local businesses to worldwide enterprises. Ensuring positive customer service can differentiate between successful and unsuccessful businesses. Customers are more likely to choose a company that provides quality service, and they will recommend that company to others.

Understanding Customer Needs and Expectations

Providing excellent customer service starts with understanding customer needs and expectations. The best way to do this is by creating a customer profile that includes details such as age, gender, education level, and lifestyle. Additionally, businesses must strive to understand the customer's expectations, including what they expect from the business. When businesses make an effort to anticipate their customers' needs and go the extra mile to fulfil them, they are building strong relationships with customers.

The Impact of Poor Customer Service on Business

Poor customer service can be detrimental to a business's reputation. Negative reviews from disappointed customers can discourage potential customers from taking their chances with the business. In addition, customers who receive poor service may turn to competitors, resulting in lost revenue.

The Role of Customer Service in Building Customer Loyalty

Building customer loyalty is one of the essential goals of any business. By building strong relations with customers and providing exceptional customer service, businesses can cultivate loyal customers that ultimately benefit their bottom line. Investing in customer service promotes customer loyalty, which can help to ensure a business's continuous growth.

Common Customer Service Challenges

There are several challenges that businesses face when providing customer service. These challenges include dissatisfied customers, difficult inquiries, and complaints or negative reviews about products or services. There may also be language barriers or miscommunication between the business and customers due to differences in dialect or accent.

The Need for Continuous Improvement in Customer Service

Providing exceptional customer service is not a one-time event but an ongoing process. Regularly reviewing customer feedback and identifying areas where improvements can be made is essential to providing an excellent customer experience. As businesses grow and evolve, so do their customers' needs and expectations, and businesses must constantly adapt and improve their customer service to meet these expectations.

Key Skills Required for Providing Excellent Customer Service

Providing excellent customer service requires a range of skills, from strong communication to problem-solving abilities, to a deep understanding of the customer's needs. Employees must be trained to deliver an exceptional customer service experience. They must be friendly and approachable, capable of actively listening to customers, and find ways to provide solutions to meet their needs.

Setting Customer Service Goals and Measuring Success

Setting customer service goals and regularly measuring success is essential for providing excellent customer service. Establishing customer satisfaction targets and measuring staff performance can help businesses identify areas for improvement and identify opportunities for providing better customer service solutions. Consistently tracking metrics like customer satisfaction, wait times, and issue resolution times can provide insight into the areas that need improvement. Setting realistic goals and tracking key measurements can help businesses make Customer Service a priority throughout the organization.

In summary, providing exceptional customer service is essential for any business's success. Understanding customer needs and expectations, addressing common challenges, investing in employee training and measuring satisfaction rates are some of the key takeaways from Chapter 1. In the following chapters, we will delve deeper into how to execute Customer Service strategies that can maintain and grow customer loyalty.

CHAPTER 2: CREATING A CUSTOMER-FOCUSED CULTURE

A company's culture holds a significant role in building and maintaining great customer service. Companies that foster and promote a culture of customer service excellence are more likely to meet and exceed their customers' expectations. A customer-focused culture involves strategies that prioritize customer satisfaction and convenience as the most critical factors for a business. This chapter will offer strategies for building a culture that is entirely dedicated to exceeding customer expectations.

Importance of creating a customer-focused culture

Building a culture that is entirely dedicated to customer service is essential in creating the perfect business environment for customers. If every employee is invested in offering superb customer service, then that will reflect positively on the company culture. The environment of a business is created by its employees, who are responsible for the consumer's attitude towards the brand. A customer-focused culture involves aligning the company values with the customers' needs, and every employee should strive to provide the best experience possible for them.

Building a culture of customer service excellence

Creating a culture of customer service excellence involves developing a set of principles and values that align with the company's overall mission to provide the best customer experience. Employee training, rewards, and recognition programs are effective ways of creating a culture that is fully dedicated to customer satisfaction.

Training employees on customer service best practices

Training employees on customer service best practices in an essential strategy in building a customer-focused culture. It is essential to ensure that every employee, no matter their role, understands that customer service is an essential factor in the company's mission. Training should be comprehensive, offering relevant information on the best customer service practices, customer feedback and complaints handling procedures.

Empowering employees to make decisions to benefit customers

Empowering employees to make decisions to benefit customers is vital in creating a culture that prioritizes customer satisfaction. By allowing employees to make decisions related to customer service, you reduce bureaucracy and promote creativity in solving customer problems. Empowering employees to make decisions is essential in creating an environment where quick resolutions to customer issues can be achieved.

Encouraging employees to be proactive in addressing customer needs

Encouraging employees to be proactive in addressing customer needs is a crucial aspect of customer service. Employees should always endeavor to be attentive, anticipate the customers' needs, and provide quick solutions to any issues they face. Being proactive in addressing customer needs is crucial in offering outstanding customer service and creating a customer-focused culture.

Fostering a culture of open communication and feedback

Fostering open communication and feedback in a company is essential in creating an environment dedicated to customer service. Employees need to be encouraged to express their views on customer service matters, share best practices and offer feedback on areas that need improvement. Honest communication about customer service issues helps identify areas of improvement, fosters creativity, and promotes a culture that is fully dedicated to exceptional customer service.

Recognizing and rewarding employees for exceptional customer service

Recognizing and rewarding employees for exceptional customer service is an important strategy in building a customer-focused culture. An effective recognition program involves acknowledging employees who deliver consistent and excellent customer service. Recognition could include bonuses, public acknowledgment, promotions, and even training programs. Rewarding and recognizing employees for exceptional customer service encourages them to continue delivering excellent customer service and foster a customer-focused culture throughout the organization.

Aligning company values with customer needs

Aligning company values with customer needs is crucial in creating a customer-focused culture. If the organization prioritizes its values over customer needs, then it is unlikely to meet customer expectations fully. Organizations should strive to ensure that their values align with the customer's priorities and create a culture that explicitly reflects this. When the company is entirely focused on meeting customer needs and expectations, the business is more likely to thrive and succeed.

Conclusion

Creating a customer-focused culture entails aligning company values with customer needs, recognizing, and rewarding exceptional customer service, empowering employees to make decisions that benefit customers, fostering open communication and feedback, fostering a culture of customer service excellence, training employees on customer service best practices, and encouraging employees to be proactive in addressing customer needs. Building and fostering a customer-focused culture is crucial in maintaining excellent customer service and contributes to the overall success of a business.

CHAPTER 3: COMMUNICATING EFFECTIVELY WITH CUSTOMERS

Effective communication is the foundation of great customer service. How you communicate with your customers can make or break even the most well-planned approach to customer service excellence. Communicating effectively is not just about speaking clearly – it also relies on other factors like listening actively, showing empathy, and responding to customer inquiries promptly.

Importance of effective communication in customer service

In most companies, customer service representatives are usually the first point of contact for customers. Effective communication sets the tone for the interaction and establishes a connection with the customer. Once a customer feels heard and understood, they are more likely to be patient and receptive to your solutions, even if they don't entirely resolve their issue. Effective communication can also build trust and promote customer loyalty, as it shows the customer that you are genuinely interested in helping them.

Types of communication channels available to customers

Today's customers expect multiple channels of communication to be available to them – phone, email, chat, text, social media, and more. Each channel has its unique advantages, but they all require different communication styles. For example, if a customer calls, they prefer a more personalized approach with an empathetic voice, whereas an email might require a more formal tone.

Understanding customer language and preferences

It's essential to tailor your communication style to match the customer's preferred language, tone, and style. Some customers might prefer a more relaxed, friendly approach, while others might want a more professional and straight-to-the-point interaction. Knowing your audience and taking the time to understand their preferences can help build rapport and trust with your customers.

Active listening and responding to customer inquiries

Active listening is a vital skill in effective communication. Paying attention to the customer during an interaction demonstrates that you value their time and input. It also helps you fully understand the issue they are facing – ensuring that the solutions you offer meet their needs. When responding to customer inquiries, it's important to be prompt but also thorough. Addressing all their concerns and questions will give them the confidence that their issue is being handled properly.

Handling difficult or angry customers with professionalism

Customer service representatives are going to face difficult or angry customers, no matter how good the service is. It's essential to handle these situations with professionalism and composure. Understanding the customer's perspective is crucial. It might not be apparent why they are angry, but there's usually a valid reason behind their behavior, which can sometimes stem from a previous bad experience. Responding patiently, actively listening to the customer, and taking their point of view into account can improve the conversation's trajectory.

Using positive language to build rapport with customers

Positive language sets an upbeat tone and helps to build rapport with customers. It's essential to use language that elevates the customer and focuses on solutions, rather than problems. Positive language can start as early as a simple greeting, like "Good morning," "How can I assist you?" Listening carefully to the customer's words and replying with appropriate positive language phrases can also promote meaningful and friendly conversations.

Responding promptly to customer messages and requests

Prompt and efficient responses to customer messages and requests are essential in modern customer service. Customers expect swift resolution, and possible delays can lead to frustration and even worse customer experiences. Answering customer messages quickly ensures that they feel acknowledged and valued. It's better to have up-to-date technology and software that will help you automatically respond to messages with customer queries.

Providing clear and accurate information to customers

Providing clear and accurate information is vital in any business, but it is especially important within customer service. Your customers contact you because they need help with something – it's likely they don't understand the issue or how to resolve it. A clear, concise, and accurate explanation of the solution must be communicated effectively to ensure that they have everything they need to resolve their issue. Additionally, providing clear information when a solution is not immediately available helps the customer understand what is happening, and when they can expect a resolution.

In conclusion, effective communication is crucial to achieving great customer service. It helps to establish trust and build relationships with customers. Customer service representatives must be trained to listen actively to understand the customer's perspective, to use clear and positive language, and to respond promptly and provide accurate information. Effective communication is the backbone of providing excellent customer service.

CHAPTER 4: BUILDING RAPPORT WITH CUSTOMERS

In a world where customers have endless options to choose from, building a strong rapport with them has become critical for businesses. It's not enough to just provide great products or services, businesses must establish a lasting connection with its customers to ensure repeat business.

Why is building rapport important?

Rapport is built on mutual trust and understanding. It's a feeling of connection, familiarity, and ease that is established through good communication and positive interaction. When customers feel a sense of comfort with a business or its employees, they are more likely to return, become loyal customers, and even refer others. Building rapport is not just important for the immediate transaction, but for building long-term relationships that lead to business growth.

Empathy and understanding customer perspectives

Empathy is the ability to understand and share the feelings of another person. It's a critical skill for building rapport because it allows employees to connect with customers on a deeper level. To build empathy, employees should put themselves in the shoes of the customer and understand their perspectives. By understanding their needs and wants, employees can suggest solutions that are tailored to the customer, making the interaction feel more personalized.

Personalizing interactions with customers

Personalization is key to building rapport with customers. When employees take the time to personalize interactions, customers feel valued and appreciated. Personalization can include addressing customers by name, asking about their preferences, and suggesting products or services that complement their needs.

Developing emotional intelligence to connect with customers

Emotional intelligence is the ability to identify and manage your own emotions while also recognizing the emotions of others. It's a valuable skill for building rapport because it allows employees to anticipate how a customer may be feeling and adjust communication accordingly. By showing empathy and understanding, employees can create a positive and meaningful connection with customers.

Using humor and empathy to build rapport

Humor can be a powerful tool for building rapport because it can break down barriers and create a positive and relaxed atmosphere. By using humor, employees can create a connection with customers that is unique and memorable, making them feel at ease and comfortable. However, humor should always be used appropriately and should never offend or insult the customer.

Building trust with customers through honesty and integrity

Trust is critical for building rapport with customers. Customers must feel comfortable and confident in a business and its employees to continue doing business with them. By being honest and transparent, employees can build trust and show customers that their interests are a priority.

Anticipating customer needs and suggesting solutions proactively

By anticipating customer needs and suggesting solutions before they ask, employees can build rapport and show customers that they are valued. Anticipating needs can include suggesting products or services based on previous purchases or understanding upcoming events or needs. By proactively suggesting solutions, employees can create a connection that goes beyond the immediate transaction.

Going above and beyond to exceed customer expectations

Exceeding customer expectations is critical for building lasting relationships. By going above and beyond, employees can create a positive and memorable impression that customers will remember. For example, offering a personalized recommendation or providing exceptional customer service can create a sense of loyalty and trust that can lead to future business.

In conclusion, building rapport with customers is a critical component of providing great customer service. By understanding customers' perspectives, personalizing interactions, showing empathy, using humor appropriately, being honest and transparent, anticipating needs, and exceeding expectations, businesses and employees can establish a lasting connection that fosters trust and loyalty. When customers feel valued, they are more likely to continue doing business with a company, which can lead to long-term business growth.

CHAPTER 5: MANAGING CUSTOMER EXPECTATIONS

Managing customer expectations plays a vital role in ensuring customers remain satisfied with the goods or services they have received from a business. Customers come to businesses with a set of expectations already in mind. Expectations vary in size and complexity, but customers commonly have certain expectations that they expect a business to meet. These might include timely delivery, product quality, or the overall customer experience. When expectations are not met, it can result in customer dissatisfaction and ultimately impact the business's reputation negatively. Therefore, businesses must manage their customer's expectations effectively to retain them.

Setting realistic expectations for product or service delivery

One way to manage customer expectations is by setting realistic expectations for product or service delivery. This is essential since customer's disappointment might stem because the business over-promised something in terms of delivery timelines. For example, suppose a product takes an average of five days to deliver. In that case, the business should communicate that information to customers, so they know what to expect rather than telling them it will take two days when that's not possible. Businesses can offer customers faster delivery, but these should be optional, and customers should be communicated to that they come at an extra charge.

Communicating effectively about timelines and process

Beyond setting realistic expectations for delivery, businesses should also communicate effectively about timelines and processes. This means providing customers with accurate timelines and explanations of what to expect throughout the entire process. This is important because any deviation from the declared timeline or process can lead to customer dissatisfaction. Communication can be done through different channels such as email, social media, chat, or phone calls.

Providing updates to customers throughout the process

Providing updates to customers throughout the process helps set expectations continuously and makes customers feel valued. For example, if a product takes longer to be delivered than initially anticipated, customers should be informed of the delays and the new expected delivery date. If there are any changes in the product delivery process, customers should be informed promptly to avoid surprises. In short, customers prefer to remain up-to-date on the status of their orders to help manage their expectations.

Managing customer expectations during periods of high demand

Periods of high demand can impact the business's ability to meet customer expectations. Customers might have to wait longer than usual for product delivery, experience delays in customer service, and so on. Businesses must prepare for such periods of high demand by being honest with their customers upfront. They should communicate any potential delays and the reason behind them. By doing so, they can manage customer expectations, resulting in less dissatisfaction when they experience those delays. It also helps businesses work on potential solutions to avoid high-demand problems in the future.

Handling customer complaints and addressing expectations

Managing customer expectations should not only be addressed before the sale, but also when handling complaints. When a customer files a complaint, it's the business's responsibility to address their concerns and expectations. In doing so, the business should take ownership of the problem. If the issue is with delivery, for example, explain the reasons for the delay and relay the new expected delivery date. The objective is to help the customer feel that their concerns are being heard and addressed. Addressing customer expectations helps build customer confidence and leaves a positive impression.

Providing transparency and honesty about limitations or constraints

Businesses should always be transparent about their limitations and constraints. When a product or service is not feasible, due to limited resources or other constraints, these should be communicated to the customers. Customers appreciate honesty, and when they know what to expect, they can adjust their expectations accordingly. It's essential to find solutions to the problems posed by limitations and constraints, but in the meantime, customers appreciate being told the truth.

Ensuring consistency in meeting customer expectations across all touchpoints

Meeting customer expectations is not solely dependent on one company's department or employee. Businesses should ensure that the customer experience, in terms of meeting expectations, is consistent across all touchpoints. This includes store representatives or call center employees. Each employee should possess the required knowledge and skills to provide excellent customer service and manage expectations. It's important that the business sets clear expectations and processes that are understood by everyone.

In conclusion, managing customer expectations is a vital part of excellent customer service. Setting realistic expectations for product or service delivery, ensuring consistency in customer service across touchpoints, and effectively communicating with customers throughout the process helps businesses in managing customer's expectations. By doing so, businesses can help increase customer satisfaction, loyalty, and make their customers feel valued.

CHAPTER 6 - RESOLVING CUSTOMER COMPLAINTS

Customers are the lifeline of any business. They are what keep the business running and growing, providing revenue and word-of-mouth referrals. Therefore, it goes without saying that resolving customer complaints should be the highest priority for any business. Not only is it important to address individual complaints, but it is also important to learn from them to continuously improve the overall customer service experience.

The Importance of Resolving Customer Complaints

One of the main reasons why resolving customer complaints is so important is that it has a direct impact on customer loyalty. Customers who have a negative experience are more likely to share their experience with others, leading to a decrease in potential new business. Conversely, customers who have a positive experience are more likely to become repeat customers and recommend the business to others.

Additionally, customers who have a complaint that is resolved quickly and effectively tend to have a higher degree of loyalty than those who never had a complaint in the first place. When a customer has a problem and a business goes out of their way to solve it, the customer feels more valued and appreciated. This can lead to increased loyalty and even advocacy.

Understanding the Root Cause of Customer Complaints

Before you can resolve a customer complaint, it is important to understand the root cause of the problem. This means taking the time to actively listen to the customer and ask targeted questions to gather more information. Sometimes, what appears to be a simple complaint may actually have a more significant underlying issue that needs to be addressed.

Once the root cause of the complaint has been identified, it is important to acknowledge the customer's frustration and show empathy. Apologizing and indicating that you understand the inconvenience caused can go a long way in easing a customer's negative emotions. Remember, the customer's experience of the situation is just as important as the complaint itself and should not be dismissed.

Handling Complaints with Professionalism and Respect

It is important to address customer complaints with professionalism and respect. It can be easy to become defensive or dismissive when hearing a complaint, but it is important to remain calm and listen to the customer's perspective. Avoid interrupting and allow the customer to express themselves fully.

Use positive language and try to reframe the complaint to identify the issue in a more positive light. For example, if a customer is complaining about the long wait time in a restaurant, reframe the complaint to acknowledge the popularity of the restaurant and suggest options to alleviate the wait time, such as offering appetizers or drinks before the meal.

Offering Solutions to Customer Problems

Once the issue has been identified and understood, it's time to offer solutions. Whether it is through a refund, replacement product, or other compensation, it is important to offer a solution that will resonate with the customer. Be sure to explain the solution clearly and provide any necessary information. Discuss any next steps and timelines and follow through on your promises.

Following Up with Customers to Ensure their Issue was Resolved

It is important to follow up with customers after their complaint has been addressed. This will ensure that they are satisfied with the solution, that there are no further issues, and that the customer feels valued. This can be as simple as a phone call or email checking in on their experience. It's also an opportunity to ask for feedback on how the situation was handled and if there are any suggestions for improvement.

Learning from Customer Feedback to Improve Future Service

Addressing customer complaints not only resolves the current issue but it also helps to identify opportunities for improvement in future service. When addressing complaints, it's important to collect feedback and analyze it for trends and patterns. Listen to suggestions for improvements and consider incorporating them into future policies and procedures.

On a regular basis, analyze complaints to identify the most common issues being reported, frequency, and how quickly they are resolved. Take that information back to your employees and create a process that will ensure the avoidance of those issues or finding preventive measures in case they happen again. This will help avoid any issues in the future, improve customer satisfaction, and increase business performance.

In conclusion, resolving customer complaints is essential in maintaining the satisfaction and loyalty of customers towards any business. Successfully handling complaints can change a dissatisfied customer into an advocate who will share positive experiences with other customers, leading to growth and profitability for the business. By focusing efforts and resources on providing great customer service, businesses can improve the overall customer experience and achieve long-term success.

CHAPTER 7: ANTICIPATING CUSTOMER NEEDS

Customer service isn't just about responding to customer needs when they arise, but it's also about proactively anticipating what your customers might need and offering solutions before they even ask for it. By being proactive, you not only enhance the customer experience, but you also build customer loyalty. In this chapter, we'll discuss how to anticipate customer needs and offer personalized solutions to exceed their expectations.

1. Develop a deep understanding of customer preferences

To anticipate customer needs, you need to have a deep understanding of your customers and what they value. This requires gathering data on customer behavior, preferences, and purchasing history. For example, if you're a coffee shop owner, you might notice that a significant percentage of your customers order a latte with almond milk. By knowing this, you can anticipate customer needs and ensure that you always have almond milk in stock.

Apart from data, customer feedback is a valuable source of information that can help you understand what customers like and dislike about your business. By listening to feedback, you can identify patterns and make decisions that cater to customer needs.

2. Proactively suggest solutions to customers' problems

Anticipating customer needs involves being attentive to what customers might need and offering them solutions to their problems. For instance, if you're a clothing store owner, a customer who's purchasing a winter coat might appreciate recommendations for snow boots that match the coat they are buying.

Sales associates should be proactive in anticipating customer needs and have the knowledge of the products they offer that best fits a specific customer's preference or requirement. This kind of attention and personalization can increase customer satisfaction and drive sales.

3. Personalize interactions to meet individual customer needs

Each customer is unique, with different preferences and tastes. Anticipating customer needs requires personalization to cater to each customer's individual requirements. You can use customer data and feedback to personalize interactions and offer tailored solutions. Personalized interactions can include addressing customers by their name or remembering their previous purchases and preferences. Personalization shows that you value and respect the customers' individuality and that they are not just another number.

4. Identifying opportunities to upsell or cross-sell products or services

Anticipating customer needs not only improves customer satisfaction, but it also presents an opportunity for businesses to upsell or cross-sell products or services. Customers are more likely to purchase additional products or services when personalized recommendations are offered.

For example, if a restaurant is known for their steaks, they might offer a wine pairing that complements the steak to a customer who's ordering their favorite steak. By understanding customer preferences, you can offer supplementary products or services that meet their specific needs.

5. Using data and analytics to predict customer behavior

Data analytics can be used to identify patterns and trends in customer behavior. By analyzing data, businesses can predict customer behavior and cater to their needs accordingly. For instance, a mobile phone company could prompt customers to purchase a charger when they're running low on battery life based on an algorithm that predicts when a customer will run out of battery life.

By leveraging predictive analytics, businesses can identify customer needs before they indicate them—leading to a more exceptional customer experience.

6. Applying marketing techniques to better understand customer needs

Marketing techniques can help businesses better understand customer needs by identifying trends and patterns. By using marketing methods, businesses can learn more about customer preferences, behaviors, and trends.

For instance, if a business is monitoring their social media accounts, they may see customers asking for a particular product or service that's currently not available. By identifying such needs, businesses can plan accordingly and avoid customer dissatisfaction.

7. Staying current on industry trends and best practices to anticipate future needs

It's essential to stay current on industry trends and best practices to anticipate customer needs. By keeping up to date with the latest developments in your industry, you can stay ahead of the curve and be proactive in meeting customer needs.

For instance, if a business owner was running a technology company, they would need to be aware of the latest technology trends to anticipate customers' future needs and adapt accordingly.

Conclusion

Anticipating customer needs is a crucial aspect of providing exceptional customer service. By understanding customer preferences, personalizing interactions, and using data to predict customer behavior, businesses can offer solutions proactively, create a positive customer experience, and build customer loyalty.

By continually working on anticipating customer needs, businesses demonstrate their commitment to providing the best possible service. As a result, customers are more likely to trust and stay loyal to businesses that provide proactive customer service.

CHAPTER 8: MAKING A GREAT FIRST IMPRESSION

The proverb, "You never get a second chance to make a first impression" is certainly true in the business world. As a customer, the moment you walk into a store or walk up to a business, your first impression begins to form. A good first impression is critical in building customer loyalty and ensuring repeat business. So, how can you make a great first impression?

Creating a Welcoming Environment for Customers

The first thing customers notice about your business is the physical appearance of the storefront or office. Therefore, it is crucial to creating an inviting and welcoming environment for customers. Here are some tips to keep in mind:

❖ Cleanliness: Keep the physical appearance of your store or office clean and clutter-free. Dust shelves, wipe down counters, and sweep the floors regularly. No customer wants to walk into a dirty environment.

❖ Lighting: Good lighting can enhance the appearance of your storefront or office. Bright lighting can draw customers in and make them feel welcome whereas dim lighting can create a dull and uninviting atmosphere.

❖ Layout: The layout of a store or office can impact the

perceived size and openness. Make sure to keep the space organized and easy to navigate, with clear signage to help customers find what they are looking for.

- ❖ Design: Displaying products or decorating in a way that showcases your business's style and personality can give customers a sense of the company's values, creating a lasting impression.

- ❖ Atmosphere: The type of music played, scent (if any), and temperature of the space can impact a customer's comfort level and overall impression of the business.

Greeting Customers with a Smile and Positive Attitude

When a customer walks into a store or office, the first thing they will notice is how they are greeted. Therefore, it is essential to train your employees on the importance of a warm greeting. This initial interaction sets the tone for the rest of the customer's experience.

Welcoming customers with a smile and positive attitude can make them feel more comfortable and trusting of the business. The tone of voice and body language displayed by the employee also should be conveyed in a warm and friendly manner.

Personalizing Interactions with Customers during Their First Visit

A personalized greeting can make a massive difference in creating a great first impression. Asking for the customer's name, thanking them for choosing your business, and personalized recommendations based on the customer's interests can make them feel valued and important.

Building Trust through Clear and Honest Communication

Customers are encouraged to put their trust in your business when they know upfront that your communication is honest and transparent. Being open with customers helps create a sense of trust and respect for your company.

If there are any limitations or constraints to the products or services offered by the business, be sure to communicate this to customers up front. Also, avoid making promises that the business cannot keep; honesty is always the best policy.

Providing Helpful Information to Customers

Customers appreciate businesses that can provide information about products, services, and promotions available. Being informative and providing useful information can also help create a great first impression.

Letting your customers know about any special promotions or discounts available in-store or online can make them feel special, creating a lasting positive impression.

Following Up with Customers after Their Initial Visit

It is always a good practice to follow up with customers after their initial visit to see if there is any feedback you can use to improve their overall experience. There are several ways to follow up with customers, including email, phone calls, or text messages.

Follow-up messages show customers that your business cares about their experience and would like to hear from them. It also gives them an open platform to communicate any comments, concerns, or areas where they think your business can improve.

Conclusion

Making a great first impression is a critical element in providing excellent customer service. It takes several elements to work together, including having a welcoming environment, greeting customers with a smile and positive attitude, personalizing interactions, building trust through clear and honest communication, providing helpful information, and following up with customers after their initial visit. By doing these simple things, your business will create a lasting positive impression that customers will remember for years to come.

CHAPTER 9: TRAINING EMPLOYEES ON CUSTOMER SERVICE BEST PRACTICES

Providing excellent customer service is a crucial goal for any business that wants to thrive and succeed in the long-term. And while your company may offer remarkable products or services, it's ultimately the quality of your customer service that will determine whether people stay loyal to you or choose to take their business elsewhere. That's why it's critical to invest in training your employees on customer service best practices to ensure that they can deliver high-quality experiences consistently.

Identifying Areas Where Employees Need Additional Training

Before you start training your employees, it's important to identify areas where they may need additional support. Start by observing your employees' interactions with customers to see how they typically respond in different situations. Take note of any areas where you see room for improvement or where employees might seem unsure or uncomfortable.

You could also consider running customer satisfaction surveys to gather feedback directly from your customers about the quality of service they've received. This feedback can be a valuable tool in identifying areas where employees need extra training and support. You could also use mystery shopping services to simulate customer experiences, which can be helpful if you can't observe your employees firsthand.

Providing Ongoing Training to Keep Employees Up-to-Date on Best Practices

Training isn't a one-off event, but rather an ongoing process that requires your commitment and investment. To provide high-quality customer service, it's essential to keep your employees up to date with the latest best practices and techniques. You could provide regular training sessions for employees to refresh their knowledge and learn new skills.

You may also want to consider hosting refresher courses for your employees to ensure they are implementing the latest customer service practices. Think in terms of annual training sessions for improving customer service and incorporate ongoing education or training programs that can be accessed throughout the year.

Incorporating Customer Service Training into New Employee Onboarding

Customer service training should be an essential part of your company's onboarding process for new employees. From their first day on the job, employees should be familiarized with the importance of customer service in the company culture. In addition, new hires should be given comprehensive training on customer service best practices to ensure they get off to a good start in providing high-quality customer experiences.

Reinforcing the Importance of Customer Service Excellence Regularly

It's crucial to create a service-oriented culture that encourages employees to prioritize customer satisfaction. Reinforcing the importance of customer service excellence regularly is an effective way to ensure that customer service remains a top priority for all staff members.

Regular meetings, reminders, and other training sessions can be helpful in keeping your employees focused on delivering high-quality customer experiences. You could also consider implementing a customer service incentive program to reward employees who excel in customer service.

Using Real-life Scenarios to Train Employees on Handling Difficult Situations

It's valuable to use real-life scenarios to train employees on handling difficult customer situations. Create a simulated environment and ask employees to handle complaints and issues in as close to a real-world context as possible. This will give employees the chance to practice their customer service skills in a safe environment.

The ability to handle difficult situations calmly, empathetically, and effectively can be a game-changer when it comes to building customer satisfaction. By preparing your employees for any scenario, they'll be better equipped to handle customers who may be angry, upset, or simply dissatisfied.

Encouraging Employees to Share Their Own Customer Service Success Stories

Encouraging your employees to share their own customer service success stories can be a great way to promote a positive team spirit centered around customer satisfaction. Highlighting employees who have gone the extra mile in providing exceptional customer service can be a great way to inspire other employees to follow suit.

Create an internal forum where employees can share their experiences with one another and promote a culture of continually striving for excellence in customer service. Recognizing and celebrating great customer service can go a long way toward motivating your team and building a customer-oriented culture.

Recognizing and Rewarding Employees Who Excel in Customer Service

Finally, it's crucial to recognize and reward employees who excel in providing outstanding customer service. By acknowledging employees who go the extra mile for customers, you create a culture that values service excellence, which can lead to motivated and satisfied employees.

Recognition need not be in the form of monetary rewards. You could offer verbal praise, a certificate, or even a mention in the company newsletter. Regularly acknowledging and rewarding exceptional customer service can help your employees feel valued and motivated, leading to better job performance over time.

Conclusion

Providing great customer service is a skill that can be acquired, refined, and continuously improved through the right strategies, training, and support. Investing in employee development by providing ongoing training, implementing mentorship, or coaching programs, and recognizing exceptional customer service are all key components to achieving service excellence. By prioritizing customer service excellence, you can create a culture that is committed to satisfying your customers and ensuring your company's long-term success.

CHAPTER 10: EMPOWERING EMPLOYEES TO MAKE DECISIONS

If you want to provide exceptional customer service, you need to empower your employees to make their own decisions. This means giving them the training, resources, and guidelines they need to act on behalf of the customer. In this chapter, we will explore why empowering employees is so important, and how you can do it effectively.

The Importance of Empowering Employees

Empowering employees to make decisions is critical for several reasons. First, it enables your employees to react quickly to customer needs. When customers have a problem, they don't want to wait around for a manager to make a decision. They want their issue resolved quickly and efficiently. Empowering employees to make decisions gives them the ability to address customer needs on the spot, without having to wait for approval from a supervisor.

Second, it improves employee satisfaction and engagement. When employees feel empowered, they feel trusted and valued. This can enhance their motivation and job satisfaction. When employees are happy, they are more likely to provide excellent customer service. Conversely, when employees feel powerless, they may become disengaged and disenchanted.

Third, empowering employees can reduce costs and increase efficiency. When employees are empowered to make decisions, they can resolve customer issues faster, without having to escalate them to a higher-up. This can reduce the workload of managers and supervisors, freeing them up to focus on other tasks.

Guidelines for Empowering Employees

While empowering employees can have many benefits, it's important to do it correctly. Here are some tips for empowering employees to make decisions:

- ❖ Provide clear guidelines: Empowerment doesn't mean that employees can do whatever they want. You need to establish clear guidelines and expectations for decision-making. Outline what decisions employees are authorized to make and how they should handle situations that fall outside of their authority.

- ❖ Train employees: Proper training is critical for empowering employees to make decisions. Make sure they understand the company's policies and procedures and give them the skills they need to solve customer problems effectively.

- ❖ Encourage ownership: Encourage employees to take ownership of customer issues. Give them the responsibility and authority to resolve problems on their own. This will instill a sense of pride and commitment in their work.

- ❖ Provide resources: Give employees access to the resources needed to make informed decisions. This could include access to customer data, technology tools, and product manuals.

❖   Encourage judgment: Encourage employees to use their judgment in solving customer issues. When employees are given the freedom to think on their feet, they can come up with creative solutions to problems.

❖   Recognize and reward employees: Acknowledge employees who make effective decisions. Celebrate their successes and reward them for their efforts. This can motivate employees to continue providing exceptional customer service.

❖   Use feedback to improve: Use employee feedback to continuously improve decision-making processes. Ask for their input and listen to their suggestions for improvement. This can help you refine your approach to empowering employees.

Conclusion

Empowering employees to make decisions is essential for providing great customer service. It enables your employees to act quickly and effectively on behalf of the customer, enhances employee satisfaction and engagement, and can reduce costs and increase efficiency. By providing clear guidelines, training employees, encouraging ownership, providing resources, encouraging judgment, recognizing, and rewarding employees, and using feedback to improve, you can effectively empower your employees to make customer-focused decisions.

CHAPTER 11: PROVIDING CONSISTENT CUSTOMER SERVICE ACROSS ALL CHANNELS

In today's digital age, customers expect to receive support and interact with brands through a variety of channels, including email, chat, social media, and phone. As their preferences change and new channels emerge, it's important for businesses to ensure that they provide a consistent level of customer service across all touchpoints. In this chapter, we'll explore how to achieve consistency, and why it's so important for building customer relationships and loyalty.

Coordinating Customer Service Efforts Across All Touchpoints

Providing excellent customer service is not just about having one exceptional representative who goes above and beyond; it's about providing a consistent experience across all touchpoints. When customers interact with different representatives, they should receive the same level of professionalism, knowledge, and support, no matter which channel they use.

One way to ensure consistency is to create a standard operating procedure for customer interactions that outlines best practices for each channel. This could include scripts for phone calls, response times for email and chat, and escalation paths for resolving issues. Once you have a process in place, you should train your customer service representatives, so they all have the same knowledge and expectations.

One of the most important things to keep in mind when coordinating customer service efforts is to have clear communication between all teams. Whether it's your social media team, the chat representatives, or the phone support team, make sure everyone knows the same information to prevent misinformation and confusion. Continually monitor these channels and make sure everyone is on the same page, to ensure consistency in messaging and tone of voice.

Aligning Customer Service With Overall Brand Positioning

It is important to ensure that your customer service efforts are consistent across all channels, not just in message, tone, and response times, but also in the way they align with your overall brand. Your customer service team is an extension of your brand, and should embody the same values, tone, and personality.

To bring this consistency to life, create branding guidelines and training materials that are focused on customer service. These guidelines should include voice and tone guidelines that align with your overall brand, so when your customers speak to a customer service representative, they get a clear sense of your company's mission and values.

Providing the Same Level of Service Regardless of the Channel

Customers interact with brands across multiple channels, so it's essential to get this right. You need to provide the same level of service whether they contact you through social media or reach out to the support team through email.

The key to providing consistency is to offer the same quality of response and resolution, regardless of the channel. Customers should not be penalized because they choose to interact with your brand through a particular channel. Continually monitor service levels, escalations, and interactions and make sure the same quality is provided across all channels.

Adapting to New Communication Channels as They Emerge

As new communication channels emerge, businesses need to adapt and embrace them. While there are many different channels, it's important to be aware that not every channel may be suitable for your business. Analyze the channels that your customers are already using to interact with you and determine if there are other channels that they might find beneficial.

Once you have identified new channels, it's important to ensure that your customer service representatives have the necessary skills and training needed to provide support. You may even need to create new standard operating procedures and scripts to ensure consistency across all channels.

Incorporating data and analytics into your customer service strategy can help you understand which channels are being used the most and could give you insight on potential new channels to be tested.

Handling Customer Inquiries Through Multiple Channels Simultaneously

Providing customer service across multiple channels can be overwhelming, which is why it's important to implement a customer service platform that allows for managing multiple channels. This kind of software can help customer service reps manage requests and inquiries and keep track of everything in one place. This ensures that conversations across channels are effortless, and everyone is up to date to provide timely and accurate responses.

Some tools offer the additional functionality needed to monitor customer satisfaction across multiple channels, to provide a better understanding of what's working and what may need improvement and puts all the data together to have a more comprehensive analysis of how customer support is being handled.

Using Data to Identify Areas Where Consistency Could Be Improved

Data is one of the most valuable assets in customer service because it can give you insights into how your customer service team is performing and how it can improve. By analyzing data on each channel, you can identify areas where customers may experience issues or challenges.

For example, perhaps you've noticed that customers who submit support tickets are frequently transferred to multiple representatives before finally receiving a resolution. This data shows that you may need to restructure your customer service teams or implement additional training to ensure that representatives are better equipped to handle inquiries independently.

Final Thoughts

Providing consistent customer service across all channels is key to building trust and loyalty with customers. It may take some effort and coordination, but the benefits of providing a seamless experience are worth it. By aligning customer service efforts with your overall brand messaging, adapting to new channels, and using data to identify areas for improvement, you can create a customer-centric experience that ensures customer loyalty and, in turn, business growth.

CHAPTER 12: MEASURING CUSTOMER SATISFACTION

Customer satisfaction is one of the most important indicators of the success and health of your business. It not only helps you identify areas for improvement but also enables you to celebrate success and build customer loyalty.

Measuring customer satisfaction is essential for any business that wants to provide excellent customer service. It helps identify areas that require attention, enabling you to improve your processes, enhance the customer experience, and build better relationships with your customers.

Understanding the Different Ways to Measure Customer Satisfaction

The first step in measuring customer satisfaction is to understand the different ways in which you can do it. The two most common methods are surveys and feedback mechanisms.

Surveys are questionnaires that ask customers about their satisfaction levels. They can be sent via email or included in website pop-ups.

Feedback mechanisms, on the other hand, are tools that allow customers to provide feedback about their experiences, such as chatbots and comment sections on social media platforms.

Tracking Customer Feedback in Real-Time

Real-time tracking of customer feedback is critical as it allows you to respond quickly to customer feedback. It also enables you to identify patterns in customer behavior and preferences.

Online tools can help you collect feedback from customers in real-time. For instance, if you sell products online, you can use a survey tool to ask customers about their satisfaction levels after they make a purchase.

Collecting Data Through Surveys and Other Methods

Surveys are one of the most commonly used methods to collect data about customer satisfaction. They are designed to gather customer feedback on different aspects of your business, including product quality, customer service, and overall satisfaction.

Other methods for collecting data include call monitoring, social media monitoring, and focus groups. By using these methods, you can get a more comprehensive understanding of customer opinions and needs.

Identifying Key Performance Indicators for Customer Service

Identifying the key performance indicators (KPIs) for customer service is important as it helps you understand the specific areas that require attention. KPIs can include metrics such as customer retention rate, response time, and resolution time.

Once you have identified the KPIs for customer service, you can use them to measure your success in meeting customer needs and expectations. You can also use these KPIs to create goals for improving your customer service.

Using Data to Identify Areas for Improvement

Data is crucial for improving your customer service. By analyzing customer feedback and tracking KPIs, you can identify areas that require improvement and make data-driven decisions on how to make those improvements.

For instance, if you notice that customers are experiencing long wait times during customer support calls, you can analyze the data to identify the root cause of the issue. Once you identify the cause, you can implement changes to reduce wait times and improve the customer experience.

Incorporating Customer Feedback into Business Decisions

Once you have collected customer feedback and analyzed the data, it is vital to incorporate that feedback into your business decisions. By doing this, you can ensure that your business is meeting customer needs and expectations.

For instance, if customers consistently complain about the complexity of your sign-up process, you can simplify your process to accommodate their needs. Not only will this enhance the customer experience, but it will also help to improve customer satisfaction levels.

Celebrating Successes and Making Improvements Where Necessary

It is essential to celebrate successes and make improvements where necessary. When customers are happy with your service, it is important to recognize and appreciate their loyalty. By doing so, you can build customer loyalty and encourage repeat business.

Additionally, when areas of improvement have been identified, make the necessary changes to ensure that your business is meeting the needs of your customers. Continuously monitoring and making improvements is crucial for providing excellent customer service.

Conclusion

Measuring customer satisfaction is a critical aspect of providing excellent customer service. By understanding the different ways to measure customer satisfaction, tracking customer feedback in real-time, and identifying key performance indicators for customer service, you can identify areas that require attention and prioritize your efforts to improve customer satisfaction levels.

By using data to identify areas for improvement, incorporating customer feedback into business decisions, and celebrating successes while making improvements where necessary, you can continuously improve your customer service and build stronger relationships with your customers.

CHAPTER 13: USING TECHNOLOGY TO ENHANCE CUSTOMER SERVICE

Technology has revolutionized the way businesses operate and interact with customers. It has enabled businesses to provide quick and efficient service while also reducing the workload on customer service representatives. In this chapter, we will explore how technology can be used to enhance customer service.

Deploying Chatbots and Virtual Assistants to Handle Customer Inquiries

Chatbots and virtual assistants are being used by businesses to handle customer inquiries. These programs are designed to mimic human-like conversations and can provide quick answers to customer inquiries, freeing up customer service representatives for more complex issues. Chatbots can be programmed to provide information about products, services, or even process transactions, such as booking appointments or ordering products.

Automating Routine Customer Service Tasks to Free Up Human Resources

Automating routine customer service tasks, such as password

resets or order tracking, can free up human resources for more complex customer inquiries. Automation can also provide customers with self-service options, such as accessing their account information or resolving their own customer service issues.

Using Data Analytics to Personalize Customer Interactions

Data analytics can be used to personalize customer interactions. By analyzing customer data, businesses can provide customized recommendations and offers based on their preferences and behavior. Personalized interactions can increase customer satisfaction and loyalty, which in turn can lead to increased sales and revenue.

Providing Customers with Self-Service Options

Customers prefer self-service options and businesses can provide self-service options through their websites, mobile apps, or social media pages. Self-service options save customers time and allow them to access support services in their own time and at their own pace.

Using Customer Relationship Management (CRM) Software to Manage Customer Interactions

Customer Relationship Management (CRM) software provides businesses with a central location to manage customer interactions. This software allows businesses to track customer interactions and provide a personalized experience for each customer. CRM software also provides businesses with analytics to help them improve customer service and manage customer relationships.

Ensuring Seamless Integration with Other Systems and Platforms

To ensure that technology is providing efficient customer service, it is important that different systems and platforms are integrated seamlessly. Customers should be able to access the same information on different platforms, and customer service representatives should have access to all the relevant customer information.

Monitoring Technology Performance and Making Improvements Where Necessary

It is important to monitor the performance of technology and make necessary improvements to ensure that it is providing efficient customer service. Monitoring technology performance can help businesses identify any weak points and make necessary improvements to enhance customer service.

In conclusion, technology is a crucial tool that businesses can use to enhance their customer service. By deploying chatbots and virtual assistants, automating routine tasks, personalizing interactions, providing self-service options, managing customer interactions with CRM software, ensuring seamless integration, and monitoring technology performance, businesses can enhance customer satisfaction and loyalty. Technology can help businesses provide efficient customer service while also providing more personalized experiences for customers.

CHAPTER 14: BUILDING CUSTOMER LOYALTY

In today's highly competitive business world, customer loyalty is one of the most important goals for any organization. It is much more cost-effective to maintain existing customers than to acquire new ones. The loyalty that customers feel towards a business not only helps to build brand reputation and drive repeat business, but it also influences other prospective customers.

The benefits of customer loyalty are not something to be taken lightly. Research has shown that increasing customer loyalty by just 5% can lead to an increase in profits of between 25% and 95%. So, how do you build customer loyalty? The answer lies in providing exceptional customer service at every touchpoint.

Providing Exceptional Service at Every Touchpoint

Building customer loyalty starts with providing exceptional customer service at every touchpoint. The journey of a customer with a business usually begins with the very first interaction. This could be the first time a customer visits your website, calls your customer service team, or visits one of your brick-and-mortar locations.

It is important to make a great first impression by ensuring that the customer's needs are met effectively and efficiently. Ensure that your communication channels are well-staffed and provide clear and accurate information at every step.

Providing Special Offers and Promotions

One of the most effective ways to build customer loyalty is to offer rewards and incentives for your customers' repeat business. This can be in the form of special promotions, discounts, or loyalty programs. Such offers and promotions show your customers that you appreciate their business and value their loyalty.

Loyalty Programs

Customers are always looking for ways to save money and get good value for their money. Implementing a loyalty program is an effective way to reward your customers for their repeat business. With a loyalty program, customers can earn points or rewards every time they make a purchase. These rewards can then be redeemed for discounts, free products, or other special offers.

Customer Advocacy and Word-of-Mouth Marketing

Businesses that provide exceptional customer service create positive experiences that can encourage customers to share their success stories. Word-of-mouth marketing is one of the most effective tools for building brand reputation and driving repeat business. Encourage your loyal customers to share their experiences and use their feedback to improve your business.

By providing exceptional customer service, you create advocates for your business. These advocates can promote your business, products, or services to new customers. According to a Nielsen survey, 92% of consumers trust recommendations from friends and family above all other forms of advertising.

Consistently Delivering on Brand Promises

To build customer loyalty, it is important to establish a reputation for consistent delivery on your brand promises. If customers have a positive experience with your business, they are more likely to return and recommend your business to others. Consistency in your services, communication, and products creates a trust factor that your business stands for quality.

To deliver on brand promises, it is important to align your customer service with overall business strategy. Ensure that the management and employees understand the importance of customer service and work together to consistently deliver high-quality services.

Conclusion

Building customer loyalty is fundamental to the success of any business. The benefits are clear; loyal customers are more likely to remain with the business and recommend it to others. Providing exceptional customer service is key to building customer loyalty. By understanding the needs of your customers and delivering on your brand promises, businesses will attract and retain loyal customers. Encourage feedback, embrace customer advocacy and word-of-mouth marketing, and create reward systems. These are some simple ways to build long-lasting relationships with your customers.

CHAPTER 15: CREATING A POSITIVE CUSTOMER EXPERIENCE

In today's increasingly competitive marketplace, providing a positive customer experience is more important than ever. Gone are the days where offering good customer service was enough. Customers now expect a seamless and personalized experience across all touchpoints. A positive customer experience can lead to increased customer loyalty, positive word-of-mouth marketing, and increased revenue for your business. In this chapter, we'll examine the key components of creating a positive customer experience.

Understanding the Difference between Customer Service and Customer Experience

To create a positive customer experience, it's important to understand the difference between customer service and customer experience. Customer service refers to the individual interactions that customers have with your business, such as speaking with a customer service representative on the phone or in person. Customer experience, on the other hand, refers to the overall impression that customers have of your business based on all of their interactions with your brand. This includes things like your website, social media presence, customer service interactions, and the quality of your products or services.

Providing a Seamless and Consistent Experience

Customers expect a consistent experience across all touchpoints. This means that they should be able to seamlessly transition from one channel to another without having to repeat themselves or provide redundant information. For example, if a customer contacts your business via email, they should be able to follow up with a phone call without having to repeat their issue. To provide a seamless and consistent experience, it's important to have a customer relationship management (CRM) system in place that can track customer interactions across all channels.

Understanding Customer Needs and Preferences

To provide a positive customer experience, it's important to understand your customers' needs and preferences. This means taking the time to listen to customer feedback and incorporating it into your business practices. You can gather customer feedback through surveys, social media, or by simply asking customers directly. Once you have an understanding of what your customers want and need, you can tailor your customer experience to meet those needs.

Offering Personalized Interactions and Solutions

Customers expect personalized interactions and solutions. This means using data and analytics to personalize customer interactions, offering customized solutions to customer problems, and anticipating customer needs before they arise. Personalization can take many forms, such as offering personalized recommendations based on past purchases or addressing customers by name in emails. By offering personalized interactions and solutions, you can create a memorable customer experience that will keep customers coming back.

Anticipating Customer Needs and Exceeding Expectations

To provide a truly exceptional customer experience, you need to go above and beyond customer expectations. This means anticipating customer needs before they arise and providing solutions proactively. For example, if a customer has an issue with a product, you could proactively offer a replacement or refund before the customer even asks. By exceeding customer expectations, you can create a positive and memorable experience that will keep customers coming back.

Providing a Memorable Experience

Providing a memorable experience is key to creating a positive customer experience. This means creating a unique and personalized experience that customers will remember long after their interaction with your business is over. Memorable experiences can take many forms, such as offering special promotions or discounts, sending personalized thank you notes, or offering customized product recommendations. By providing a memorable experience, you can create customer loyalty and positive word-of-mouth marketing for your business.

Using Customer Feedback to Continuously Improve the Customer Experience

To provide a positive customer experience, it's important to continuously improve your customer service practices. This means using customer feedback to identify areas for improvement and making changes to your business practices accordingly. By making continuous improvements, you can stay ahead of the competition and provide a truly exceptional customer experience.

In conclusion, providing a positive customer experience is essential for businesses in today's competitive marketplace. To provide a truly exceptional customer experience, it's important to understand the difference between customer service and customer experience, provide a seamless and consistent experience across all touchpoints, understand customer needs and preferences, offer personalized interactions and solutions, anticipate customer needs, and exceed expectations, and provide a memorable experience. Continuously using customer feedback to improve your customer service practices is also crucial to providing a positive customer experience long-term. By embracing these key principles, you can create a customer experience that will keep customers coming back for more.

CHAPTER 16: DEVELOPING A CUSTOMER SERVICE STRATEGY

Customer service is an essential aspect of any successful business. The customer experience plays a crucial role in determining whether customers return or recommend the business to others. To ensure that your company is providing the best possible customer service, it is essential to have a well-planned customer service strategy. In this chapter, we will discuss the key elements of developing a customer service strategy.

Understanding the Company's Vision and Mission for Customer Service

The first step in developing a customer service strategy is to understand the company's vision and mission for customer service. This involves understanding what your company wants to achieve in terms of customer service and why it matters. A clear vision and mission statement will guide your customer service strategy and help you to focus on the outcomes that matter most.

Setting Clear and Measurable Customer Service Goals

Once you have a clear understanding of your company's vision and mission for customer service, the next step is to set clear and measurable customer service goals. These goals should be specific, achievable, and relevant to your company's overall business objectives. For example, you may aim to reduce customer wait times or improve customer satisfaction ratings.

Identifying Resources Required to Achieve Customer Service Goals

To achieve your customer service goals, you will need to allocate the necessary resources. This may include additional staff, training, and technology investments. You may also need to reallocate resources from other areas of your business to support your customer service goals.

Conducting Research on Customer Needs and Preferences

To provide excellent customer service, you need to understand your customers' needs and preferences. Conducting customer research through surveys, focus groups, and social media can provide valuable insights into what your customers want. Analyzing this data can help identify trends and areas where you can improve your customer service.

Defining the Customer Service Experience You Want to Provide

With a clear understanding of your customer needs and preferences, you can define the customer service experience you want to provide. This includes identifying the key touchpoints where your customers interact with your business and developing a plan to deliver a positive customer experience consistently across all channels.

Aligning Customer Service Strategy with Overall Business Strategy

It is essential to align your customer service strategy with your overall business strategy. This ensures that your customer service goals are consistent with your business objectives and that your customer service initiatives support your company's growth and success.

Communicating Customer Service Strategy to Employees and Stakeholders

Once you have developed your customer service strategy, it is essential to communicate it to your employees and stakeholders. This ensures that everyone in your organization understands the importance of customer service and the role they play in delivering exceptional customer service. Communication also fosters a culture of customer service excellence and can help to build support for your customer service initiatives.

In Conclusion

Developing a customer service strategy is essential to providing excellent customer service and building customer loyalty. It involves understanding your company's vision and mission for customer service, setting clear and measurable goals, identifying resources, conducting research on customer needs and preferences, defining the customer service experience you want to provide, aligning your customer service strategy with your overall business strategy, and communicating your customer service strategy to employees and stakeholders. With a clear customer service strategy in place, your business can build a reputation for exceptional customer service and enjoy sustained success.

CHAPTER 17: HIRING AND RETAINING TALENTED CUSTOMER SERVICE STAFF

One of the most critical components of providing excellent customer service is hiring and retaining talented customer service staff. Hiring the right people for customer service positions is crucial because customer service representatives are the face of your brand and the first point of contact for customers. Retaining customer service staff is just as important because it takes time and effort to train new hires and build a customer-focused culture.

Identifying Key Skills and Traits

To hire the right customer service staff, it's crucial to identify the key skills and traits required for excellent customer service. Good customer service requires a combination of technical skills and soft skills. Technical skills include knowledge of the product or service being offered, familiarity with customer service tools and technologies, and strong communication skills. Soft skills include listening skills, empathy, patience, and the ability to remain calm and professional in difficult situations.

Developing Job Descriptions and Recruitment Strategies

Once the key skills and traits have been identified, job descriptions and recruitment strategies can be developed to attract top talent. Job descriptions should clearly outline the skills and experience required for the role, as well as the expectations for the position. Recruitment strategies should be designed to target candidates who possess the skills and traits required for the role. Social media, job fairs, and employee referrals can be effective recruitment channels.

Providing Competitive Salaries and Benefits

To attract top talent, organizations need to offer competitive salaries and benefits. Compensation packages should reflect the level of experience and expertise required for the role, as well as the company's commitment to customer service excellence. Benefits such as health insurance, retirement plans, and flexible work arrangements can also be effective in attracting and retaining top customer service staff.

Providing Ongoing Training and Development Opportunities

One of the most effective ways to retain customer service staff is by providing ongoing training and development opportunities. Investing in employee training not only helps employees improve their skills but also demonstrates the company's commitment to their personal and professional growth. Regular training and development opportunities can also help employees stay up-to-date on emerging customer service trends and technologies.

Creating a Positive and Supportive Work Culture

A positive and supportive work culture is essential for retaining talented customer service staff. Employees who feel valued and supported are more likely to remain with the company and provide exceptional service to customers. A supportive work culture can be created by fostering open communication, providing opportunities for team building, and recognizing employee achievements.

Offering Opportunities for Career Advancement and Growth

One way to retain talented customer service staff is by offering opportunities for career advancement and growth. Providing a clear career path for customer service employees demonstrates the company's commitment to their professional development. Promoting from within the organization can also help build a customer-focused culture and retain top talent.

Recognizing and Rewarding Outstanding Employee Performance

Recognizing and rewarding outstanding employee performance is another way to retain top customer service staff. Recognizing exceptional customer service can be as simple as a "thank you" note from management or a public display of appreciation. Offering incentives such as bonuses or gift cards can also be effective in motivating customer service employees to provide exceptional service.

Conclusion

Providing excellent customer service requires hiring and retaining talented customer service staff. Identifying the key skills and traits required for excellent customer service, developing job descriptions and recruitment strategies, providing competitive salaries and benefits, offering ongoing training and development opportunities, creating a positive and supportive work culture, offering opportunities for career advancement and growth, and recognizing and rewarding outstanding employee performance are all critical components of hiring and retaining top customer service staff. Building a team of dedicated and skilled customer service representatives is essential for creating a customer-focused culture and achieving long-term success in the industry.

CHAPTER 18: USING CUSTOMER FEEDBACK TO IMPROVE SERVICE

Customer feedback is a crucial tool for any business that wants to provide excellent customer service. Feedback helps businesses understand how their customers perceive their products or services and identify areas for improvement. Continuously improving customer service ensures that customers are satisfied and remain loyal to your business. In this chapter, we will discuss the importance of using customer feedback to improve your customer service.

Collecting Customer Feedback

Collecting customer feedback is essential to improving customer service. There are various methods to collect feedback, including surveys, social media, reviews, and focus groups. It's important to collect feedback through multiple channels to get a complete picture of customer opinions.

Surveys are an effective way to collect customer feedback. Surveys can be distributed through various channels, including email, website, and social media. It's essential to keep the surveys short and straightforward to encourage participation.

Social media is an excellent platform for customers to share their opinions on your products or services. Monitoring social media platforms regularly can help you identify issues and opportunities for improvement.

Reviews are also a great source of customer feedback. Encouraging customers to leave reviews on platforms like Yelp, Google, and Facebook can give you valuable insight into their experiences with your business.

Focus groups are another method to collect customer feedback. A focus group is a group of customers that provide feedback on a specific aspect of your business. Focus groups typically involve a moderator and can be conducted in-person or online.

Analyzing Customer Feedback

Once you gather customer feedback, you need to analyze it to identify trends and patterns. Analyzing customer feedback can help you understand what aspects of your business are performing well and what needs improvement.

Identifying Areas for Improvement

Customer feedback can help you identify areas in your business that need improvement. Analyzing customer feedback can help you identify specific areas where your customers are having issues. Once you identify these areas, you can take steps to improve them.

Making Changes Based on Customer Feedback

Making changes based on customer feedback is crucial to improving customer service. Once you identify areas for improvement, you need to make changes to address these issues. It's essential to communicate these changes to your customers and employees to ensure that everyone understands how you are improving customer service.

Communicating Changes to Customers and Employees

Communication is key to making improvements based on customer feedback. You need to communicate changes to your customers and employees to ensure that they understand how you are addressing their concerns. It's essential to communicate these changes through various channels to reach your customers effectively.

Monitoring the Impact of Changes on Customer Satisfaction

Once you make changes based on customer feedback, you need to monitor the impact of these changes on customer satisfaction. Monitoring customer satisfaction can help you understand how your customers perceive your business after you make changes.

Using Feedback to Inform Product or Service Development

Customer feedback can also inform product or service development. It's essential to listen to your customers' needs and preferences to create products or services that meet their needs. Feedback can help you identify opportunities to innovate and differentiate your business from your competitors.

Conclusion

Using customer feedback to improve customer service is crucial to ensuring customer satisfaction and loyalty. Collecting customer feedback, analyzing it, and making changes based on the feedback are essential steps to improving customer service. It's essential to communicate these changes to your customers and employees to ensure everyone understands how you are improving customer service. Continuous improvement ensures that your customers remain satisfied and loyal to your business.

CHAPTER 19: ADDRESSING CULTURAL DIFFERENCES IN CUSTOMER SERVICE

In today's global marketplace, businesses are serving customers from all walks of life and cultural backgrounds. Because of globalization, it is essential for companies to understand cultural differences and design customer service interactions that align with these differences to cater to their diverse customer base. Addressing cultural differences in customer service is crucial for building long-lasting relationships and enhancing customer loyalty.

Understanding how cultural differences can affect customer expectations:

Culture plays a significant role in people's communication styles and behaviors, and it also impacts their expected level of customer service. It is important to note that cultural differences are manifested in various forms like expectations, beliefs, values, norms, etiquette, and language. In Customer service, a comprehensive understanding of various cultures to establish the desired customer service is imperative. For instance, in some cultures, it is customary to engage in small talk before getting to the matter at hand, while others prefer a more straightforward approach. Similarly, in some cultures, eye contact is a sign of honesty or confidence, while in others, it is interpreted as disrespect. Therefore, it is crucial to have a basic understanding of cultural differences to prevent any misunderstandings and provide excellent customer service.

Identifying common cultural differences in customer service:

There are several cultural differences to keep in mind when designing your customer service approach. Some of the most common include:

❖ Communication Style: Some cultures prefer direct communication, while others prefer indirect communication. For instance, in Asian countries, customers may not directly express their complaints or displeasure, but rather through subtle cues. To provide the best customer experience, you should be aware of these differences in communication styles and adapt your approach accordingly.

❖ Language: Language barriers are prominent when working with customers from different cultural backgrounds, it is highly recommended to provide multilingual customer service to cater to your diverse customer base. It is also essential to understand the nuances of language to avoid any linguistic misunderstandings.

❖ Etiquette: Different cultures have different etiquettes, so keeping that in mind can be beneficial in providing excellent customer service. For instance, bowing is a part of the culture in some Asian countries, as a sign of respect, so it is crucial to take note of those nuances, especially when serving customers from those countries.

❖ Time: Customers from different cultures have different attitudes towards time. For instance, in some cultures, it is customary to be early for appointments while in other cultures, showing up on time is acceptable.

Training employees on cultural awareness and sensitivity:

It is essential to train your employees in cultural awareness and sensitivity to prevent any cultural misunderstandings that may occur in customer interactions. Providing cultural sensitivity training helps employees to build a better understanding of customers from diverse cultural backgrounds and enables them to provide excellent customer service. The training should focus on the following:

❖ Basic cultural awareness: Employees should be able to identify key cultural differences in communication styles, values, and norms in their interactions with customers.

❖ Effective communication: Employees should learn to adapt their communication style to align with each customer's needs and preferences.

❖ Multilingual support: Providing customer service in multiple languages will help ensure that employees can assist customers from diverse cultural backgrounds.

❖ Tools and resources: companies designed a cultural handbook that helps the employees familiarize themselves with the culture of the client countries.

Adapting customer service practices to meet the needs of different cultures:

Adapting your customer service approach to cater to different cultural preferences can lead to better customer satisfaction and build long-lasting relationships. Some strategies to adapt your customer service practices include:

❖   Support for different languages: Provide multilingual customer service support to cater to different customers communicating in different languages.

❖   Customizing Interactions: Adapting the customer service interactions as per the specific customer requirements can also be fruitful results in customer satisfaction otherwise consider it as a blanketed approach that works everywhere but not the best anywhere.

❖   Personalization: Personalizing the customer service interactions and experiences to align with individual customer preferences.

❖   Planning ahead to address cultural differences: Plan ahead and anticipate customers' cultural differences to ensure that the customer service approach used aligns with those differences.

Celebrating and respecting cultural differences in customer service interactions:

Celebrating and respecting cultural differences in customer service interactions helps build strong relationships with customers and enhances customer loyalty. Embracing diversity can create a sense of belonging for customers, which motivates them to shop more often and recommend the business to others. Celebrate cultural differences with holidays, greetings, and celebrating different customs adhered to within different cultures and this enhances your customer's experience and satisfaction.

Conclusion

Cultural sensitivity is a crucial aspect of providing excellent customer service in today's diverse business environment. Understanding cultural differences, training employees on cultural awareness and sensitivity, adapting customer service practices to meet the needs of different cultures, and celebrating and respecting cultural differences in customer service interactions are key to building long-lasting relationships with customers, enhancing customer satisfaction, and promoting customer loyalty. Expanding your business globally is possible with these considerations put in place to cater to the customer base in each country and culture.

CHAPTER 20: CONTINUOUS IMPROVEMENT IN CUSTOMER SERVICE

Customer service is a dynamic field, and businesses must continually evolve their practices to meet customer needs and stay ahead of competitors. Without continuous improvement, businesses risk falling behind in providing exceptional customer service. In this chapter, we will explore the importance of continuous improvement in customer service and outline strategies for achieving it.

Measuring Performance Regularly and Setting Improvement Goals

One of the essential components of continuous improvement in customer service is measuring performance regularly and setting clear improvement goals. This involves tracking metrics such as customer satisfaction, response time, and employee performance. By monitoring these metrics regularly, businesses can identify areas where improvement is necessary and develop strategies to address them.

Setting clear improvement goals is crucial to the success of any continuous improvement effort. These goals should be specific, measurable, and achievable within a defined timeframe. Businesses should determine the key performance indicators (KPIs) relevant to their operations and set targets for improvement. For example, a business may set a goal of reducing customer wait times by ten percent within the next six months.

Encouraging Feedback from Both Customers and Employees

To achieve continuous improvement in customer service, businesses must encourage feedback from both customers and employees. Customer feedback can be gathered through surveys, social media, or other channels. This feedback provides valuable insights into customer expectations, preferences, and pain points. By analyzing this feedback, businesses can identify areas for improvement and make necessary changes.

Employee feedback is equally important. Employees are the frontline representatives of a business and have unique insights into customer needs and preferences. Encouraging employees to provide feedback on customer service practices, processes, and tools can help businesses identify areas where improvements can be made.

Identifying Areas Where Improvements Can Be Made

Continuous improvement in customer service requires a willingness to identify areas where improvements can be made and a commitment to making necessary changes. This can involve analyzing customer feedback, conducting customer surveys, or benchmarking against industry standards. Businesses can also leverage technology to help automate tasks, streamline processes and provide better customer service.

Experimenting with New Approaches to Customer Service

Businesses must be willing to experiment with new approaches to customer service. This can involve adopting new technologies or re-envisioning traditional customer service practices. Experimentation is essential because it helps businesses find new and innovative ways of meeting customer needs and expectations.

Learning from Industry Trends and Best Practices

To stay ahead of the competition, businesses must learn from industry trends and best practices. This involves regularly reviewing industry research, attending conferences and events, and networking with industry peers. By staying abreast of industry trends and best practices, businesses can identify new opportunities for growth and improvement.

Investing in Technology and Training to Improve Customer Service

Investing in technology and training is a critical component of continuous improvement in customer service. Technology can help businesses automate tasks, streamline processes, and provide better customer service. Training employees on the latest customer service best practices and tools can also help ensure that they are equipped to meet customer needs and expectations.

Making Customer Service a Priority Throughout the Organization

Finally, to achieve continuous improvement in customer service, businesses must make customer service a priority throughout the organization. This involves ensuring that all departments and employees understand the importance of customer service and are committed to providing exceptional customer service at every touchpoint.

Conclusion

In today's competitive business environment, providing exceptional customer service is critical to the success of any business. Continuous improvement in customer service requires a commitment to measuring performance regularly, encouraging feedback from both customers and employees, identifying areas where improvements can be made, experimenting with new approaches to customer service, learning from industry trends and best practices, investing in technology and training, and making customer service a priority throughout the organization. By following these strategies, businesses can provide exceptional customer service that meets the needs and expectations of their customers.

Final Thoughts

Great customer service is the lifeblood of any successful business. It's not just about making sales; it's about building relationships and creating a loyal customer base that will continue to support your business for years to come.

Remember, customers want to feel valued and appreciated. They want to know that their concerns are being heard and addressed in a timely manner. By providing exceptional customer service, you can meet these needs and surpass their expectations.

Throughout this book, we've explored various strategies and techniques for providing great customer service. From active listening to timely follow-ups, each tactic is designed to help you build trust with your customers and foster a positive reputation for your business.

But the journey doesn't end here. Great customer service is an ongoing effort that requires constant attention and dedication. By staying attuned to your customers' needs and continuously improving your approach, you can create an experience that keeps them coming back time after time.

So go forth with confidence, armed with the knowledge and skills necessary to deliver truly exceptional customer service. Your business and your customers will thank you for it.

ABOUT THE AUTHOR

Ray Goodwin

Ray Goodwin, is the author behind this series of captivating books on Business Development and self improvement, and has left an indelible mark on the field. He was born and raised in the bustling city of London, where he developed a strong work ethic and an insatiable curiosity about the inner workings of successful businesses. Throughout his illustrious career, Ray leveraged his extensive knowledge and experience to help numerous companies flourish and prosper.

His keen insights and innovative strategies has earned him recognition, driving him to share his expertise with others. Ray believes in the power of sharing knowledge to elevate businesses and empower aspiring entrepreneurs.

Ray's dedication to his craft is evident in the numerous books he has authored on business development and self improvement. His writing style seamlessly blends practical advice, thought-provoking concepts, and real-life case studies, making his books invaluable resources for business professionals and novices alike. His ability to distill complex concepts into accessible language has greatly impacted the lives and careers of countless individuals.

Now retired from the corporate world, Ray and his beloved wife have settled in the idyllic English countryside. Surrounded by the beauty of nature, Ray finds inspiration for his writing and indulges in his hobbies.

Ray Goodwin's books continue to serve as enduring guides for those seeking success in the business world. With a wealth of experience and a deep understanding of the inner workings of businesses, Ray's work remains a testament to his passion for sharing knowledge and helping others flourish.

www.ingramcontent.com/pod-product-compliance
Lightning Source LLC
Chambersburg PA
CBHW062358290526
45794CB00005B/2275